Scattered Showers
In a Clear Sky

Scattered Showers
In a Clear Sky

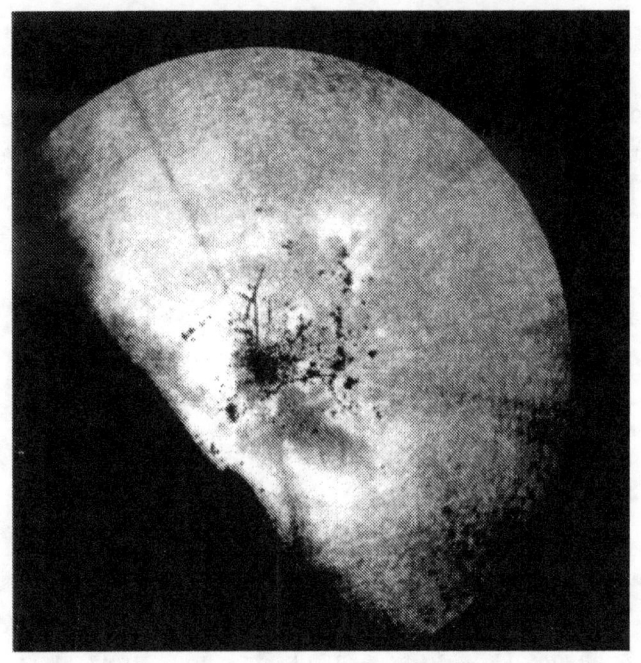

Anne Higgins

Plain View Press
P. O. 42255
Austin, TX 78704

plainviewpress.net
sb@plainviewpress.net
1-512-441-2452

Copyright Anne Higgins, 2007. All rights reserved.
ISBN: 978-1-891386-81-7
Library of Congress Number: 2007929832

Cover art: *Migration #2*, Quilt, Caryl Bryer Fallert, ©1995.

Photograph, title Page: *Radar Image of Migrating Birds*, radar image of migration stopover areas, Sidney Gauthreaux, Interim Technical Report ,1999, Legacy Project.

Acknowledgements

"Untangling," *Hirschhorn Museum Publication*, May, 1997; "Joining the Circus," *Drexel Online Journal*, January 2002; "Storm Lightning, Charleston," *Windhover*, Spring, 2002; "Fixing the Lock," *Windhover*, Spring, 2002; "On a Superhighway in Maryland," *The Melic Review*, September, 2002; "The Signatures on the Nests," *Windhover*, Spring, 2003; "In Medias Res," *Spirituality and Health*, Summer, 2004; "Litany of the Audubon Calendar," *Spirituality and Health*, Feb. 2005; "Scar," *The Centrifugal Eye*, Fall 2005; "Awake/Asleep," *Psycholoanalytic Perspectives*, Fall/Winter 2005; "Locator," *Scribble*, Summer, 2006; "One Word Singing," *The Centrifugal Eye*, Spring 2007.

Contents

1		7
	Iceberg	9
	Project Wind Seine, Cape May	10
	At the Kinzer Mennonite Cemetery	11
	Crop Circles	12
	On Falls Road	13
	Great Falls In July	14
2		15
	Untangling	17
	Making Tea	18
	Fixing the Lock	19
	Fabricating	20
	Finding the Dead Cat Under the Porch	21
	Tending the Fire	22
3		23
	First Grade at Saint Agnes School, 1954	25
	Riding *El Rapido*, 1970	26
	Joining the Circus	27
	Playwright and Poet	28
	Moving the Monarch	29
	Connections	30
	The First Annual Book Fair, Washington	31
	My Mother's Feet, At 91	32
	An Only Child On the Family Tree	33
4		35
	After Laughter	37
	Name Your Poison	38
	The Receiver Of the Action	40
	The End In Itself	41
	Out By the Shed	42
	Kairomone	43
5		45
	In Paradise With Mary Powell	47
	Walt's Warning	48
	Rapunzel At Midlife	49
	Georgia O'Keeffe Looks Over Her Shoulder	50
	Remedios Varo Paints "Mimesis"	51
	Moon	52

Rosa Bonheur Paints "Plowing In the Nivernais"	53
"Jack-in-the-Pulpit No. IV"	55
The Legend Of Our Lady Of Buglose	56
On a Superhighway In Maryland	58

6

	61
Weather Is the Roughest Kind Of Prose	63
Storm Lightning, Charleston	64
Hurricane Coming, Petersburg	65
Spider	66
Poison Ivy	67
The Signatures On the Nests	68
Goldfinch Mathematics	69
Connecticut Warbler Stunned On the Sidewalk	71

7

	73
Scattered Showers In a Clear Sky	75
Great Blue	76
Spring Peepers	77
The Wren	78
Redstart	79
Litany Of the Audubon Calendar	80

8

	83
One Word Singing	85
Locator	86
Paratechnics	87
In Medias Res	88
When the Secrets All Are Told	89
Talents	90

9

	91
Incantation	93
Susan died still fighting,	94
A History Of My Broken Heart	95
Scar	96
Junk Drawer	97
Curing Blindness	98
Elvis Has Left the Building	99
Awake/Asleep	100
The Daruma Doll	101
About the Author	103

1

Iceberg

An iceberg holds secrets
that nobody knows
but the dead whose ships
have encountered
those frozen mountains
in the sea.

Surely the mouse knows,
with her folded brown body,
who's wintered with her
small cocoa children
in plastic flowerpots
stacked in the garden shed
stuffed with soft
shredded lawn and leaf bags....
surely her closet-like
palace by the garden in the woods
appears like a corrugated
iceberg to the grass
which slants like waves
around its edge.

Project Wind Seine, Cape May

Barbara, in the first dim arrival
of the Alzheimers,
trods clumsily along
beside me
to the naturalist's
station.

He frees the warbler from the net,
weighs it, checks how much fat
protects the tiny body
by blowing on the feathers
and looking at the skin.

Then he hands Barbara
the Magnolia Warbler.
He puts this wonder of wind-caught
gold
caught on its way South
in her amazed hand.

She holds the bird briefly, then
opens palm,
and it flies on
to its home in
the rainforest.

At the Kinzer Mennonite Cemetery

At last, I see them.
I see them!
They are holding hands
as they rise from beneath the headstones,
pillows of their double bed.

He speaks:
*I stood where you stand,
In 1922, in March,
when the pasture grass greened,
crying, holding the week old twins,
calling to the mourners –
Can anyone take these children?
Can anyone take these children?*

*I went home with all six,
hanging on each other,
hanging on me.
How they huddled with me
on the long evenings.*

*Then the fiery truck
took me from them.
1924, and I'm bedded down
again with my love
here, where the farmland
stretches out around us.*

We rise to stare at you,
graying daughter
of our daughter.
We look across
83 years
at you,
older than we ever knew.

Crop Circles

Early in my writing career I came to believe that the stories I wrote were already written in the unconscious by a hand other than my own.
     James Lee Burke

Geometry was my worst subject,
but I love it slicing its way through the cornfield.
Flowers, mandalas, pentagrams,
twelve years now, each summer
new theorems.
Snowflakes, insects,
quilt squares,
Who speaks here?
What message whistles
in the high corn?
In the wheat, what coded words
have I been ignoring?
The cure is part of the art,
the unfolding of the origami of pain.
At the approach of the reaper,
sheaves bow down like Joseph's dream,
not cut,
but bent.

On Falls Road

At last a hint of Spring lurks in the scum,
immensity of slime and plastic slush
that promises to last a thousand years.
The pink sky shows above the JFX,
the black green distant hemlocks in the dusk.
In forty warm degrees the jug snow melts.
An old girl falls on heaved up sidewalk edge,
congratulates herself on solid bones,
on teeth intact, gloved brushburns, glasses scratched —
considering her once trustworthy feet.
When soreness creeps up from the gritty curb,
she hugs her thrift shop Roland Park wool coat.

Great Falls In July

Although the heat sinks into stone,
the roasted rocks lean toward the shade.
Where gargling water cools the blade,
where tumbling danger flanks the bone,
from deep to center, I'm alone.
I grip the rocks and feel betrayed.
Although the heat sinks into stone,
the roasted rocks lean toward the shade.
From plunge to mist the river moans.
My heart pounds fire within the glade.
I feel the spray sting all I made,
the small falls I'm ashamed to own.
Although the heat sinks into stone,
the roasted rocks lean toward the shade.

2

Untangling

Greasy yellow hose, thick as a child's arm,
blue rope thick as a dogwood trunk,
white rope grey with dirt, thick as a child's arm.

Hopeless tangle on the workroom floor,
writhing tangle on the workroom floor,
writhing serpents on the workroom floor,
distinguished by the colors of the rope,

writhing serpents on the workroom floor,
blue intestines on the workroom floor,
old sea sailings on the workroom floor,
yellow hose thick as a child's arm,
frayed and broken ends of chestnut mane
together tangled into argument
of complex sentences, equivocations,
qualifications all in a mess
on the workroom floor.

Strippers and sanders on the shelf,
unplugged witnesses of argument
say: how will it be undone?
Man attentive to untangling
stares without strategy.

Making Tea

Brownred liquid changes water into tea.
Smell the metal sweet hot smell,
feel the chuckle of steam in my nose.
Know the cradle of heat in my hand.
Drink the swallow of warmth in my throat.
Follow the map through the tunnel
by my lungs,
all the way to my molten core.

Fixing the Lock

Lock broken after years of use.
Removed from the wrench of the door
slim, tarnished as a cigarette box.
Brass, flat, it sat in the wood
like a coin in the eye of the dead.

Unscrewed from its long residence,
entirely slipping out into hand
like a secret passageway opening
smooth, silent, dust in the grease.
Six small screws loosened, removed,
clotted with timedust, oil, doordust.

Brass box opens, shows
springs, clips, buds of metal
oilblack, sandgrime,
now to the blind repair,
uncertain reassemblage.

Fabricating

The clothing did not fall from you in tatters,
nor did your feet swell these 40 years.
The Goodwill store sells everything that matters.
Forget the Lord and Taylor, all your fears
are smothered in the well worn corduroy.
The warm grey sweater sent to you with love —
each time you wear it I can feel your joy.
Reject stiff clothing, that which does not give,
the labels biting back into the neck,
the slippery polyester you once wore.
Embrace the blouse so fine it feels like silk —
the cotton blouse whose ironing was a chore.
Choose vibrant reds and purples from the rack.
Discover cashmere that the rich gave back.

Finding the Dead Cat Under the Porch

The cat had been a large grey one, I think.
Perhaps he belonged to the old man who owned the house
before us, who had lost his mind to old age,
and lost the house, too.

The space under the large
wraparound porch
was high enough to stand in.
Its earthen floor,
latticed walls,
stone walls
became his tomb,
large enough for
the pharaoh of cats.

When I ventured in
with an armful of garden tools,
I first thought he was
a cast off air conditioner filter,
or the discarded brush
of an old floor buffer.
Then I saw the round head
in the broken light through the lattice,
and understood what I
was smelling.

Salty, pungent
cat smell padded through the house,
rubbed against the walls
where the old man
had written poems in pencil
to the Snowball Cat,
Pharaoh of Cats.

Tending the Fire

Still I am in the hands of the unknown God; he is breaking me down to his new oblivion...
                    D.H.Lawrence

Don't you love a good fire?

About every ten minutes,
add a small log.
Keep feeding it.
The heat must be intense enough,
constant enough,
steady enough
to set a husky arm of oak to
burning from its core.

It's messy work.
Grit from the twigs on the polished floor,
black soot from the poker
on my hands.

My father told me how to keep a fire burning.
Now he sits in the cold winter sunlight
at the Home,
when the sooty darkness
catches the twigs of day.

I sit before the fire in the dark living room,
on the floor before the fire,
feeding it,
watching it like a TV show about my
still burning, though crumbling love.
The flames orange my face.
Roaring silence
issues from their hunger.

3

First Grade at Saint Agnes School, 1954

Linda Esslinger opens her lunch box—
lettuce, tomato. Mayonnaise smears her sandwich,
her pink mouth, her porcelain chin.
I wouldn't touch that mayonnaise.
My sandwich must be
neat and dry, nothing dripping.
In front of me stretches the clean cut neckline
of John Moore's haircut.
His clean red ears grow out from his skinny head
like snail shells.
In my plaid skirt, I lust after
Patricia Kobar's bright pink organdy dress
with fluffy full skirt, lace edged collar
studded with rhinestones.
Marie Lakatosh dupes me into giving her
my only pencil,
then jeers at me for writing with
a crayon.

How we fall out against one another.

Riding *El Rapido*, 1970

Somewhere between Lisbon
and Salamanca
in the hot, dry July,
so different from humid home,
I noticed my hair, long then,
to my elbows, felt
sleek and straight as it never was before,
and never was again.

He smoothed it, praising thick silk of it,
all spun cherrywood gold in the desert sun.
The rattling train stopped frequently.
He'd jump off and buy us wine and bread.

By sunset, we shared our third class compartment
with a famiy of six, baby crying,
chickens coughing the dry dust.

We were 22 then,
just out of college.
Everything was romance.
Our lives, *El Rapido*.

Joining the Circus

Didn't I always want to in those days
when I trudged to work in the office
in the city! Wasn't I jealous of Dorothy
in the Florida camp
where she was paid
to teach pigeons
to roller skate!

Didn't I always want to in those days
when I wore teacher clothes
and drove to work in Dundalk.
Wasn't I jealous of John
driving a carny truck
down the bandaid roads
of central Pennsylvania,
setting up the nickel pitch
at the county fairs,
arranging the pink bears.

In Baltimore,
in 1972, our roach run row house
creaked like a circus tent,
dirty clothes lay in piles
like flags,
the unclean kitchen smelled
like fried dough,
and our puppy was not housebroken.
She cried in the morning
when we went to work
like a calliope.

Playwright and Poet

The deeply satisfying sense of being spoken to privately
Patricia Hampl

Open the velvet curtain —
you have made your room a black box theater.
Styrofoam sculptures
hang from the walls
smiling down at us.
The fan whispers heat
from the heavy sidewalk.

Tell me of the plays in your mind.
Tell me of the voices of strangers,
how they move
in settings never seen before.
I will sing you my hymns to electricity,
my psalms to our entertainments.

We fell in love with being poor and young,
unknown as oysters
in a brine blind bay.

Moving the Monarch

I saw the future, four years ahead,
the bodies falling from the towers,
young people's shoes with the feet still in them,
gentle mailmen breathing death.
That's why I climbed right out of the tunnel of work
the minute she opened the cellar door.

She brought the monarch in its cocoon
from New Orleans,
brought the milkweed stem it called home
from the yard where flowers still flamed.
She brought me to the box
and showed me.

The monarch, flexing new wings,
climbed from her finger to mine.
My finger like a
milkweed stem,
a taste of salt.

The cloth on the floor of the box
offers something softened by wear,
something to cling to
on the way to
winter in the greenhouse.

Connections

Orb weaver,
shy and harmless to humans,
cast herself
down a bare basement bulb,
climbed back up,
cast a parallel line
and a cross wire between.
At the intersection
of leafmeal smell
and cellar damp,
her web is fragile
as old hands,
shiny thin skin
stretched across large blue veins.

I seat myself
in my childhood church
for my uncle's funeral.
The family stands
at the intersection, oblivious to
the oncoming traffic of wedding, baptism, and suicide.

Funnel weaver,
sheetweb,
cellar spider,
your real name is
harvestmaster.

The First Annual Book Fair, Washington

I walked there from Union Station
to the Capitol grounds
on September 8, 2001.
Cloudless blue sky blasted us with heat.
Poets sweating in the shade of the striped tents.

That was Saturday.
Monday night, I went to the library
to see the falconer and his birds.
I held the female peregrine
completely calm
on my gloved arm.
She stared into my eyes,
she had the black implacable eyes
of Mohammed Atta
on his last night on earth.
We stared into each others' eyes.

Tuesday, another blue sky,
planes accurate,
falcon fast.

My Mother's Feet, At 91

Both big toenails
grey as concrete, rough as the pumice
she used to use on her bunions.
Second toe lapped over the big toe
like a drunken buddy.
She used to call them dogs
at the end of a long day of pounding them
around the hospital wards,
dogs forced to carry
two hundred extra pounds.
Now, in the bed,
Liver brown skin
of the old worn dogs
flakes away,
gritty with the sand of
ancient sweat,
abandoned shoes.

An Only Child On the Family Tree

It's a European Mountain Ash.
Sometimes called a Rowan tree, it likes
light, peaty soil —
its pale brown wood, tough and strong,
makes tool handles, cart wheels,
the juice of its berries
heals the bowels,
its magical powers
revered by Druids.
This one came from Switzerland, though.
Sprouted from an Amish seed
rooted in Pennsylvania.

The trunk set deep aggressive roots
in Leacock township, close to Paradise,
thickened by weather and loamy earth,
the tough trunk sent out
long branches, branching out from each other
with dozens of offspring from each marriage —
Amazing in May
with its spray of white flowers.

People with no electricity,
terse and clannish,
black pants flapping on the clotheslines,
women with bare feet like cudgels,
walking behind the plough,
well tended buggies
drawn by dashing horses,
mahogany hides gleaming
along the narrow roads,

continued

one old twig
growing on an orphaned branch
of a larger branch
broken off by a long ago storm —
I'm looking for a way
for the tree to take me back.

4

After Laughter

Therefore I commend mirth;
so I praise laughter;
after all, I turn to grinning.
In the end, I prefer to chortle, to chuckle,
guffaw, snort, split my sides,
tears of mirth, earthy mirth,
rips of laughter, tides of noise, human breath gasping.
I can't cry, but I can still laugh
at slapstick,
the foot on the banana, the pie in the face, the butt on the floor —
hit, broom! slice, twig!
I commend mirth!
I award a crown of candy,
reward hilarity!
Laughing wins, winds, winding around my guts,
splashing out my open throat,
tasting so much better than bile.

Name Your Poison

Apple morsel
choked Snow White.
Belladonna, called the witch.

Bloodroot floods the forest,
cousin to monkshood, Jack in the Pulpit,
companion to crowfoot,
dogbane, Devil's trumpet —
deadly orchestra.

Back home,
the medicine cabinet
holds Dilantin, Digitalis,
chloroform.

In the kitchen,
warm wood cabinet under the sink
hides Drano, lye, bleach.

In the far corner of the basement
grey peeling shelf
supports arsenic, strychnine, malathion.

Sun flecked garden
flaunts colchium, lobelia —
Far corner of the back yard
shades lily of the valley, bleeding heart, larkspur.

Yellow stains skin
heartbeat stutters, starved of air,
muscles freeze, tongue burns
fierce convulsions, pressure plummets.

Thick blue glass bottle glints
on the counter
in an old apothecary shop.
We want it to kill a rat,
said the youngest of the three revellers.

The Receiver Of the Action

Active verbs bite better than passive ones.
They grow teeth.
The subject smiles as the Doer-Of-the-Action.
I turn the medal.
I know the church.
I resist pain.
The cheetah curls her lip.

So much more interesting to do
than to be done to.
For Lent, I give up helping verbs,
adverbs.
I say stations on the street.
I replace my old litany of the verbs to be:
appear, become, continue,
feel, grow, look, remain, seem...
with some of the million verbs to do:
applaud, berate, count,
fry, grapple, leer, reenact, squash...
words that cry for vengeance.

The End In Itself

Truth of whatever kind is the proper object of the intellect.
Newman

The nineteen-year-old
and her sixteen-year-old sister,
neither apprehend it nor contemplate it.
They have just crashed into a pole
on a twisting road
on a fair clear Friday afternoon,
and the live-wire Death descends on the car
like a Cooper's hawk, and
all is flames and flying.

The eighty-year-old philosopher meets
this same truth,
his brain consumed by the black hunger
hiding in his fair scalp,
the fruit of long walks on sunbaked roads,
the herb garden in August,
the white patio in Greece.

The blonde philosopher
walks in the sun, while the same truth lurks,
unknown to himself.
Unknown to herself the girl flies down the road
in her new car,
laughing, showing off for her sister
and the curve comes.
Apprehend this.
Contemplate it.

Out By the Shed

Fledgling squirrel
too young to climb bark,
shivers in his first fur.
Big head, eyes half closed,
thread of a tail,
skinny body,
barely furred back legs
more like frog legs —
must have fallen from some nest.

I'm nobody's mother.
There's no baby bottle
to feed him.
I think — he's weak,
food for a fox,
one less squirrel in the world
to pillage the bird seed.

But back inside,
I see his frail wild body
shivering,
huddled against the wall
of the shed.
Somewhere inside me
a small animal
chews on my guilt.

Kairomone

A subclass of pheromone — an interspecific secretion which benefits the receiver; eg, the chemical substance secreted by the predator helps the prey because the prey have evolved a defense that is induced by the presence of the chemical.
       biology online.org

At night out here, mosquitos rule the world
with magic thick as blood. They fly
the way the wild clematis sends her shoots
to choke the cultivated Bartlett pear
whose fruit is hollowed out by greedy bees.
The fox secretes her secrets in the air.
The rabbit leaps in glowworm studded dark.

The summer fan makes silver metal sounds
that drown the shouting radio outside
so outside lies obscured by inner noise.
Our hearts hold conversations just like this.
Your words are stolen by the deafening fan
of my supposings.

5

In Paradise With Mary Powell

Milton married me when I was seventeen.
He told his friends he hasted too eagerly
to light the nuptial torch.
He called our coupling a brutish congress.

After one month, I left him,
back to my only alternative – home.
Mother and Father blanched in shame,
sent me packing, back.
I bore him four children
and left him again, when I was twenty-six,
a leaving parents could not overturn,
a more permanent haven.

Walt's Warning

To touch my person to someone else's is about as much as I can stand.
        Walt Whitman

This is how life is not tragedy.
The end: his grave in the cemetery on the side of the mountain.
The beginning: his toe stepping out
onto the sidewalk in front of the dorm
in his freshman year.
The middle: the dance, the motel room, the wedding.
The flaw: brilliant impatient double self.
The fall: the virus hitching a ride on a truck out of the Congo.
Unity of time, place, action fractured.

Rapunzel At Midlife

Despite appearances, she liked the witch.
                                    Anne Stevenson

She knew she was too old
to wear her hair long.
Those wiry grey strands belonged
in a hardware store,
not springing out from under a crown.

People never saw her cry.
She couldn't cry.
Somewhere in her thirties,
the crying broke off in the keyhole
of the witch's door.

She used her friends like tickets,
so subtly that most never felt themselves
handed to the usher,
crumpled on the floor.

The witch had evil eyes, but
they sparkled like black marbles.
She lived quietly enough
in a room above the drawbridge,
feeding the crows and sending them off
like carrier pigeons.

Georgia O'Keeffe Looks Over Her Shoulder

Just when she thinks she's painted all her fear,
when bleached skulls turn to poppies red as lust,
the sound of something wild attracts her ear.

Black jacket, white soft collar curving near
the place where desert sunset turns to rust
awakens in that neck a prickling fear.

The haunches of dead lovers gleam as clear
in skulls as in the orchid's velvet crust.
Dry rattling of bone curls back her ear.

Her upswept silken hair declares the year
in shades of gray and tortoise brown as dust
just when she thought she'd painted all her fear.

Her thin pink pearl of seashell curves to hear
the desert's voice, more fierce, more dry than just
as three fine wrinkles flow down from her ear.

Such gaunt grace turns her, luscious and severe,
containing bones and orchids, fruit and crust!
Just when she thinks she's painted all her fear,
the sound of something wild attracts her ear.

Remedios Varo Paints "Mimesis"

Woman melts into the chair,
her neck and face
the chair's upholstery,
her hands, claws on the chair's claws.
Thighs and knees still there under her skirt,
calves and feet now chair limbs.

Cat watches
from a hole in the floor:
watches the
green scarf rise like a cobra
from the basket by her left claw.

One leg of the basket stand
curls a tendril
around her leg,
another
melts pliable pincers
around the basket leg.

Everything's moving.
Leg of the chair in the corner
reaches tendrils
into the closet's closest drawer.
Green clouds waft in from the cupboard.
Everything migrates across the screen.
Her body molds across the chair,
a large world-sized body change.

Moon

> Arthur Dove 1935
> National Gallery of Art

Eye anemone,
egg white,
uneven, fringed,
grey cornea,
black pupil,
blue lid,
you eclipse the green haze of
April tree
whose trunk,
long, brown,
tilted like Pisa,
connects you
to the surging earth.

Rosa Bonheur Paints "Plowing In the Nivernais"

How thick, firm, brown, lumpy the soil,
the plowed wet soil looks.
Earth brown oxen ripple their fat backs under the yoke
in the good hour before sunset,
the nevermore ground upturned.

    *

How low-voiced the longing trees,
the longing cardinal who sings his Spring song
What cheer? What cheer?
When snow still holds the forecast?

    *

My body has different ideas
than I do.
Never no, it says.
Plow the hard packed numbness.
Never no, it says to the spotted skin.
Dimly I feel a current
coursing through my center.

Never no, it says.
Always now, it says.
Chip away the hard shell,
Chunk by miserable chunk.

    *

I remember the girl's slim, small breasted body,
the fragile shoulderblades.
Never no, that honey brown hair
will furl on that smooth neck.

continued

Never no, say the heavy shoulderpads,
the short steel wool hair.
The girl is plowed under
fifty years.

      *

It's a good hour now, my body says,
within the rose glow
where the brown oxen plow.

Back in the farmhouse,
I put my hand on the dough I have mixed and kneaded.

As it begins to rise
in the silent warm kitchen,
it is smooth and alive under my hand.
Always yes, says my body
like the dough,
even at fifty years, amazingly at fifty years,
I begin to know
upturned earth,
wet and lumpy,
ready for planting.

"Jack-in-the-Pulpit No. IV"

Georgia O' Keeffe 1930

Wonderful how the petals curl
delicately at their edges.
Layers — four layers open.
Go down in
from the blue sky down
through one and two
black bordered,
green lighted,
to three,
mantle of blue black,
grey curl at the tip
like a shoulder sagging.
Down to four then,
satin black,
then,
candle flame white grey
flash of white slit
flaring from
tornado blue thumb
at the core.

The Legend Of Our Lady Of Buglose

In the upper half of the stained-glass window,
ten farmers, housewives, and a curate,
with their 1620 clothes,
look at each other
and look down
into a large hole.
One farmer leans on his hoe with his right arm,
points with his left hand.

He points to the bottom half of the window:
golden brown, rich earth hovers
and falls away
from what it has contained:
large painted statue
of the Mother and Child,
crowned and throned,
stolid as Chartres.

In the lowest left corner of the window,
large horned ox, golden brown,
crouches in profile.
His tongue licks earth from the Mother's arm.

The tour guide tells us that
a farmer, in 1620, alerted
by the strange attitude of his beasts,
discovered them digging up the statue.

It seems that she'd been buried
in 1520,
during the Wars of Religion.
The villagers didn't want
to give her up to destruction.

Container within a container
within a container,
licked clean by cattle.
Licked clean by cattle.

On a Superhighway In Maryland

after Allen Ginsberg

Sometimes I think of you, Emily Dickinson, when I am standing
in the pouring rain,
feeling my blouse cling to my back, my hair drip into my eyes.
Sometimes I think of you while eating potato chips,
and your starvation.
Sometimes I think of you when I see the oven bird make
her unobtrusive rounds
on the ground outside my kitchen window.
I am so excited to see her there that she would never understand.

In my hungry numbness, and searching for answers, I drove
onto the Beltway, dreaming of your
spare words.
What flashing lights! What cutting in! Tractor trailers sliding
by me on the left!
Lanes full of vehicles built for snow! Business women talking
on cell phones in their black sedans… and you, May Sarton,
what were you doing in the moving van?

O Emily Dickinson, I am on my way to the Carmelite cloister
where I feel your spirit,
where I glimpse your thin shoulders heaving
at the towhee in the birch,
where I hear you imitate the love song of the house wren,
so lush compared to your spare human nouns.
I brave the Beltway to go there
and you are with me in the passenger seat,
listening with me to the radio, to the songs of my youth.
Come on baby light my fire.
Why do fools fall in love?
I see you there in the passenger seat, gripping the dashboard,
surrounded by a fiery mist.

On the way to your grave in the meadow,
Sue spoke of your treasures of fruit and flower.
She said you sat in the light of your own fire.
She said, so well you knew your chemistries, that
your swift poetic rapture was like the long glistening note of a bird
one hears in the June woods at high noon but can never see.

Sit beside me here in the traffic, Emily Dickinson,
and tell me about your selections.
Who did you watch as they carried your small body out to the hill
in May covered with flowers?

It is October as we ride the Beltway in the glaring morning sun.
Emily Dickinson, what do you say about the angry red cars,
the roaring black four-wheel drives that loom behind me?

What do you say about this walled city of streaming metal
and gas fired speed?
Will the flickering brake lights
make you sink to the floor of the car, sick with vertigo?
Will the hissing of rubber on asphalt, the tumult
of a thousand engines
make you want to disappear behind the tan concrete walls?
Will we drive all day in this exhausted maze?
We'll both be burned.
Will we reach Carmel, and stroll in the lost country of prayer?
Oh, Emily, frail and sherry-eyed, lonely scribbler,
what relief did you have when the carriage stopped for you?

6

Weather Is the Roughest Kind Of Prose

The lowering sky which clutches at my face,
the clip of surly hail against the pane,
this surely is the roughest kind of prose.

Nouns and verbs wrenched out by the roots,
switched, misplaced, branches snapping,
this surely is the roughest kind of prose.

Changelings, refugees flee the melee.
Cropping chops the lilt from loveliness.
Pruned at the wrong time,
so brash, so clean, so spare, so bare of life —
don't hope for flowers here.
This surely is the roughest kind of prose.

Storm Lightning, Charleston

Juice rises in straw like bad wires,
current flash from nave to buttress,
unseemly, fallowed by whacking thunder.
Harpy's hammer against
garbage galvanized,
an old man in the alley on New Year's eve,
smashing his kitchen pot,
his household hammer.

Death in the grass,
in the sidewise rain,
birds flee to the
side turned leaves,
all their palms up.

Hurricane Coming, Petersburg

Subtle purple maple sky
fickle sticking air
slipping away from her
climbing steps from gym to classroom,
roach dance on the musty carpet steps,
roaches roaming the rolls of paper in the closet,
mottled, peeling paint,
trickle smell of sulphur detergent.

O Death, I have loved you,
but I have not slept with you.
Were you hiding there,
in the shadows on the landing?

Navy blue sky,
tornado slithering toward her
like a shearing train.

Spider

Funnel weaver marks her web
deliberately,
linking the leaves of the sweet olive
across the yard to the camellia.
On feeling the vibration of a large ant,
she dashes out, bites him,
and carries him off
to a tornado shaped kitchen.

On an August morning,
the breeze oscillates,
expands the intricate shape.
Dew shimmers on
piteous mosquitos,
trapped and crimson,

serviceable for
weary birds who
pull at the meal
planned for another,
gracious to those
who walk at dusk.

Poison Ivy

Even the hairy brown roots, tangling in the leaves I rake
away from the emerging hyacinth shoots
can give me their miserable oil.
Under the garden, the vines are entrenched,
roots networked efficiently and randomly.
Manipulative, controlling, scheming, calculating.
they leave their weeping, itching mark
on all who brush against them.
Purple tracks of it
tattoo my arms —
dotted swiss mosquito bites,
taffeta blisters —
nature's palpable designs.

The Signatures On the Nests

When the trees bare themselves
in November,
the nests emerge,
clutch the crooks, crotches,
wrists, elbows,
between the fingers,
tangle in the fine hairs
of the topmost branches.

Vacated by their tenants,
the nests cloak their names
in the camouflage of distance.

Nest watchers recognize
the signatures
in salad bowls that perch
on the brink of heavy branches
over the canal
which do not say
robin or cardinal.
Someone else,
larger and more ponderous,
down south now,
owns those.

Goldfinch Mathematics

Pianist leans into Mozart.
Music rolls out of his fingers.
Goldfinch cloud rolls toward my window.
I see tree shade
in central Salzburg.

Little hammers dance on the square, making
heart shadows of wood
on the wood floor,
black piano like a wood whale spouting.
I hear horse hooves on a hard brown road,
brown birds fly on
silk air going gray.

Eight notes the same, insistent, minor,
bruises on the mountain's back.
I hear sonnet, conversation,
see pink heat ribbons in the air like lust
from rust in the dust of the done dance.

He tilts his hair to the silence
between the two moments.
Left hand tilts to the music.
I hear blue preludes,
New Orleans heat, wet, lush and lazy,
loose vowels,
touch so casual,
such an unintended charge.

Now his hands rest on the left,
flat out on silent keys —
then they begin to murmur —
one, then together in low close harmony.
Toccata —
second melody flies in

continued

with black wings, lemon back,
quick, scalloped all at once.

Goldfinches rise in the air together —
suddenly the left hand speaks
Quickly flee into the greying air,
the quickly baring trees!
They pass the current back and forth between them.

Connecticut Warbler Stunned On the Sidewalk

Tiny brown bird stood on the sidewalk
very quiet and still,
usually elusive, rare in these parts,
flitting in the treetops.

You've made me stiff necked in the past
as I've searched for you overhead,
but here you are, patient as a Jehovah's Witness
on the doorstep,
white-ringed eyes open, alive.
You stood on your hairpin bird feet.
Cinnamon bird, yellow breast,
palm of the hand size,
sharp beak of the bug eater,
I knelt and spoke to you,
lightly touched your breast and back,
felt the marvelous touch of
fluttering wings
for only a second
and you flew a few feet
to the bushes
to finish your recovery .

7

Scattered Showers In a Clear Sky

What else looks different from far?
What you expect it to be
it is not —
four in the morning,
flurry on the radar screen,
how many miles away
in the upper atmosphere?
We need another name for that direction.
North is different on a map.

It looks like
scattered showers in a clear sky,
and so the meteorologist calls them.
How did they finally discover
that dust on the radar was
a wide band of warblers,
storm of black-throated blues,
tornado of tanagers,
powder of parulas,
blizzard of buntings?

Prothonotaries enter a preliminary statement
across the night sky.
Redstarts rush down to the new trees.

We need another name for that direction.
North is different on a map.

Great Blue

Dawn spread a sheet of satin on the glass
canal and lake and towpath in between.
My walk was interrupted by the scene
of his arrival from the marsh to grass.
I stopped stock still in case he wished to pass,
so I could watch him without being seen —
The wide-splayed yellow fingers on the green.
How could such stick straw spindles ever last,
supporting elegance of gray-blue girth?
Binoculars allowed him in my reach...
but yellow eyes at last discovered me.
A lift of neck and feather, shrug of mirth,
one blasé glance and off the grainy beach,
into the air of swallowed memory.

Spring Peepers

In Spring the frog sounds like a bird
who with his cousins curves the night
around the pond with hot blue songs
that bend the mud and send the slight
sounds shivering into the dark,
across wet pasture, black with sleep

Across the field the undulating
chorus bites through rock and mud
to say the winter yields its howling
to the tough truth's greening blood
The eyes of songbirds cut the clouds,
their silent flight to north and nest.

The Wren

Omnipotence
is foreign to the wren.
She is all present in her garbling song.
She is all knowing as she carries thin sticks to her nest box.
She is all loving in the dawn.
She is powerful in clover to the tiny bug
but the crow could swallow her,
and she would fit into my hand.
She is eager, not tense.
She is present, not passed,
She is perfect, not single,
and no helping verbs accompany her.
Her song is a breathtaking flood,
lilting, unlikely OM
to the wrenmother.

Redstart

Cooper's Hawk, my password.
With a bang on the windowscreen,
she pushes off the sill,
snowbird in her talons.

In Wardtown Virginia,
my warbler watch began
with a Redstart
perched on a picket fence
by the country garden
in the May rain.

Spattered in my mother's blood,
I pushed off
into the cold world.

Litany Of the Audubon Calendar

Eyes of the great gray owl, intent and yellow,
at the pit of the gray grooved bowl of feathers,
largest owl in the world,
whose facial disk can hear the faintest sounds,
the mouse rustling just under the new snow —

Northern saw whet owl, big as my hand,
out for the voles —
    Have mercy on us. Stay with us.

Red billed oxpecker in Africa, starling hanging
on the mane of the giraffe, brown and buff flagstones of fur,
picking out lice and ticks, cleaning and feeding at once —

Harris hawk which I carried on my forearm once at a fair,
which nests in the crotch of giant saguaro, social raptor,
favorite of falconers —
    Have mercy on us. Stay with us.

Great egrets dancing in love or dispute,
plume birds with grace feathers streaming around them,
stick black legs, feet entwined in the air—

Great egret, frog in beak, neck like a hose,
white feather smooth as leather,
mild orange beak long shears and a dime gold eye —

Sandhill cranes equal in the sky,
legs and feet so equal in length to neck and head, silhouetted —

Black-crowned night heron, cosmopolitan, wide ranging,
crowds of you nesting
wild in the wide oak branches of the bird section
of the National Zoo,
air noisy with your conversation,
    Have mercy on us. Stay with us.

Cape May warbler, rarely at Cape May,
dependent on the health of spruce stands,
eating the spruce budworm,
flying to the Bahamas and the Greater Antilles in the winter,
singing in the cemetery in Cincinnati in the spring —

Black throated green warbler, flirting in the cemetery
in Cincinnati, jewel gold , black and yellow head,
common and confiding species, long distance migrant,
lost in the cloud on the radar screen—
    Have mercy on us. Stay with us.

8

One Word Singing

Poetry is one word singing, one word singing
in the middle of the night.
Poetry sings what no one cries.
Poetry slips in between the covers of the facts.

Josephine told me
the astronauts did
take a spider with them.
She died there
in the spaceship.
Her net wouldn't hold
in the weightless air.

Josephine told me
from her hospital bed
when she could not read or walk—

but she still sang poems
in the middle of the night,
sang between the covers
of her body
retreating
to the weightless air.

Locator

At the intersection of throat and breath,
my voice clots.
At the intersection of verse and prose, grunts
a beating drum
I can feel in my gut
between stomach and spine.

In the town of my childhood,
at the intersection of High and Gay streets,
a store sold me black marble copybooks.
At the intersection of Union and Wayne,
a red convertible turned toward me.
From a window near the corner of Market and Everhart,
I could see him coming a block away.

At the intersection of Barclay and Vineyard Lane,
where July met the garbage strike,
the rats ran the streets.

At the intersection of Bull and Rutledge,
a woman stepped off the curb
on her way to the river.
At the intersection of Franklin and Center Hill,
the sirens met the soldiers.
At the intersection of Laurel and Eastern,
I fell in love with geography.

At the intersection of sense and syntax,
I visit the house of silence.
Where paradox crosses paraphrase,
I write.

Paratechnics

Umbrella near the sun — parasol.
Group of sentences expressing a
complete thought — paragraph.
Lines going the same direction
into eternity — parallel.
Saying it another way — paraphrase.
Structure beyond climbing — parabola.
Falling through the sky
with the pull cord clutched in my hand —
parachute.

What are the limits of this exercise,
its parameters?
Vertigo spins me in
emotional misalignment — parataxic.
Arranged without conjunctions,
contradictory,
the paradox lives in a pair of small silver coins—
fearsome, ferocious,
the parasite coiled
in the foot of your soul.

In Medias Res

God arrives
almost unheard,
in heavy traffic,
forever February,
forever Lent,
forever four o'clock in the afternoon,
gray and foggy.

The eyes of the downcast
can see you only
in the basement.

Tribal people change their names
at times like these.
Henceforth, call me
Interested-in-birds.
Gripped-by-God.
Lost-Reputation.
Car-Maiden.
Belly-full-of-silk.
Hand-on-the-face-of-the-Cheetah.

Fireplace inside my body,
my ravenous mouth,
black and yapping like a raven,
wary in the bare tree is
swooping down in the snow for
a stale brick of yellow cake.

You car is a garden shaper.
A dead rose bush buried under the azaleas,
bites me as I dig.

When the Secrets All Are Told

The hearing you do
shadows my day.
In your satin room,
loud is the air with my breathing,
out are the lights of my chattering.
Wheels of my energy roll
with now slowly merging voice —

Here! Were you if nothing
but inhaling eyes,
flaring nostrils,
me tugging traffic in, my chatter
scrambles and falls —

Below far fading street lights
noise of darkening cars
cold lay the roofs, the twittering sparrows
loud in our silence —

Dark and light curtains
lift the swirling wind —
Where are you? you ask.
Here, I say.
Here.

Talents

What does it mean to enter into your Master's joy?
Come. He's back,
who has new things to do,
who has yet more to say.

And what did I do while he was away?
So long away. What did I do?

What is joy made of?
Are its walls water
or slick black rock?

Some will go there
in spite of everything.
The wet wings of the grey dusky swift
in Argentina,
up in the highest place
where Argentina meets Peru,
the fine wings fly through the waterfall,
fly to its thinnest fabric and fly through it,
groping, clumsy and wet,
up the dark slick rock
and into the slice of rock
to the nest.

Come — enter your master's joy.
The master of reins, the God of rain,
the raining God, the reigning God calls.
Come,
enter into your master's joy,
into the scandalizing center of it.
My wings fly through the forgiving wall of water.
My clumsy, wet, yearning body
clambers up to it,
to the small crevice,
to the nest.

9

Incantation

Brekekekex, ko-ax, ko-ax!
                   Aristophanes, *The Frogs*

A la recherche du temps perdu...
Music that thumps inside my skin
how can what's dead return to life?
Goldenrod grows outside my door,
trillium fills my garden floor.
How can what's dead return to life?
Music of drum and thrum of strings
dance to the slice of moon above.
How can what's dead return to life?
Flycatcher tried to fly through glass.
Holding his body here, I cry,
How can what's dead return to life?
Hurricane leveled ancient oaks
heart turned to granite rough and cold,
How can what's dead return to life?

Susan died still fighting,

hands like claws,
still unwilling to say goodbye.

Yesterday was the funeral of season
and Susan —
snow in the graveyard,
us dressed up and tramping the white snow
to get to the fake lawn around her brown casket.
Roses on it like the roses in big glass bowls
at her wedding so shortly passed.
At that, I haven't had a still sob.
Can't get season's last name. Susan's name,
house quiet, main floor still,
waiting room for death, no more will Susan
skip down those stairs.

This grief is still working
so that I could actually
talk to it—
Say, *The numbing machine does not recognize*
the image of those hands—
Say, *maybe I should go back,*
do a few more training sessions,
see if it's a matter of trying,
a matter of choice.
Time will try us
who stand there in the snow by Susan's casket —
Say, *Something's wrong with the way this year's ending.*

A History Of My Broken Heart

I did not know my heart was broken,
even when the burning spread across my chest
from shoulder to shoulder
as if it had been slathered on with a wide paint brush
full of acid,
then brushed down each arm
into the pads of my hands.
Even when the pain sat me down,
I did not know I had a broken heart,
not until the x ray photo
showed me the artery
like a strangled branch on
a winter tree, the small twigs
fading into the night
of a starving dark corner
of that wondrous plum pump.
It took years for the
built-up sorrows and fears,
the plaque sticky stored-up tears
to strangle and break my heart.

Scar

Although the rain ran like a canal
in the creases of the windowsill,
more of it pouring in, filling every crevice
of the screen,
dripping down the lip's ledge to the floor,
the woman welcomed the wet of it
to her house.
She said, *There's too much danger in the sun.*
It's lied to me for years, she said,
while it crept up and turned its key in my face.

Junk Drawer

I've always had one.
Before, it contained
mittelschmertz:
loose wire,
coffee stained spoons,
wrinkled Kleenex,
lipstick,
earring backs,
tweezers,
matches,
stamps,
tops of ballpoints,
dried up erasers.

Now,
weltschmertz:
mushy cardboard,
wrinkled calendars,
lacy raisins,
waterspilled paper,
crusted nails,
paper clips,
loose change,
dusty sunflower seeds,
lens caps,
backs of pens,
old batteries.

Curing Blindness

Vertical rain shears the
dirt from the amulet
found in the garden —
how long was it there?

I know no physicians
can fill in the macular
hole in my retina —
how can they dare

to tell me to live with it?
Clutching the talisman,
feeling the stone and the round heavy gold,
reverting to magic
when medicine fails me,
I press my eye to
its unpromising cold.

Magic has failed me
and retinal experts,
for still the grey slipper
resides in my view.
I bury the amulet,
live the periphery,
mourning the wholeness
I thought I once knew.

Elvis Has Left the Building

All that is seen and unseen
by me of my own self,
when the unseen rises up
and breaks through
and the seen goes to sleep,
it's still me.
I'm driving and so disengaged
that I miss the exit.
As they say,
Elvis has left the building,
checked out,
gone elsewhere.

Awake/Asleep

Awake, the woman fears driving in snow.
Asleep, she flies out and above it.
Awake, she lurches
through traffic. *Asleep*, she walks toward
the railway tunnel. *Awake*, she grieves
grey hair asleep, tosses it long and golden.
Awake, she clutches the newspaper.
Asleep, dodges gunfire. *Awake*, she lies alone
in a small dry room. *Asleep*, she welcomes
lovers to her bed in the glade. *Awake*,
she's past conception. *Asleep*, glowing pregnant. *Awake*
skin cancer scars, hard white. *Asleep*, sleek arms
gold in the harmless sun.
Awake, she sees the plane hit the south tower.
Asleep the planes cascade their planets
on the country far away.
Awake, she grades papers.
Asleep, she watches the flood waters
reach the second floor
of the academic building.

The Daruma Doll

You paint the first eye when you make the wish.
You paint the second when the wish comes true.

O Good Luck Doll, the shrapnel in the snow
will stay in Kosovo throughout July.
God is coming up from the inside.
I wish my first eye perfect vision.

A grey footprint marks my first eye's core,
a grey cat sitting center in the field.

The third charm added when I was confirmed.
My secret brother showed up, just in time,
the one flushed down the toilet by mistake
with all the blood of my mother's tears.

To fall seven times,
to rise eight times,
life starts from now.

About the Author

Anne Higgins teaches English and Theology at Mount Saint Mary's University in Emmitsburg, Maryland. She is a member of the Daughters of Charity, and is a graduate of Saint Joseph College, Emmitsburg, the Johns Hopkins University, and the Washington Theological Union. She has had about seventy poems published, in *Yankee, Commonweal, Spirituality and Health, The Melic Review, The Drexel Online Journal,* and a variety of small magazines. Her book of poetry, *At the Year's Elbow,* was published by the Mellen Poetry Press in 2000, and republished by Wipf and Stock in 2006.

www.ingramcontent.com/pod-product-compliance
Lightning Source LLC
Chambersburg PA
CBHW071020080526
44587CB00015B/2434